Linux

Linux For Beginners

Your Step By Step Guide Of Becoming A Linux Command Line Ninja

PS: I'd like your feedback. If you are happy with this book, please <u>leave a review on Amazon</u>.

Introduction

For some time now, there has been a rising misconception that Linux is harder to use than other operating systems, with some vendors even suggesting that the OS is only suitable for users only with an interest for open source programming.

If you've encountered any problems working with Linux, and have come here to try and learn the software, there's one thing you have to understand first. This operating system is not the problem. The only issue is that it's different; different from the other operating systems you've perhaps used your entire life- just like north Americans learn to drive on the right side of the road and the UK and elsewhere, learn to drive on the left.

With this guide, I will dispel the notion that working with Linux is hard by teaching you step by step everything you need to learn about this OS, particularly the use of the command line, and also how to use that knowledge to become a master of Linux

You'll see that not only is Linux easy to use, it's also the best OS we have today.

So, if you've been desiring to understand how to use Linux and take advantage of the many opportunities that the knowledge offers, this is your guide. It will help you understand everything you need to know about Linux- right from the basics, making the requisite installations to the terminal and many other important skills.

Table of Contents

A Comprehensive Introduction To Linux

A Little Background

Originally, Linux was developed merely as a hobby project by a programmer known as Linus Torvalds in the early 1990s while at the University Of Helsinki In Finland. The project was inspired by a small Unix (an operating system) system called Minix that had been developed by professor Andy Tanebaum who used the Unix code to teach students of that university about operating systems. At that time, Unix was only used in universities for academic purposes. The professor developed Minix (a little clone of Unix) to effectively teach his students about operating systems with a bit more depth.

Linus was inspired by Minix and developed his own clone, which he named Linux.

On 5th October 1991, version 0.02- which was the first version of Linux, was announced by Linus. While this version was able to run the Bourne shell (bash)- the command line interface- and a compiler called GCC, there wasn't so much else to it.

The version 0.03 was released some time later and then the version number was bumped up to 0.10, as more people began embracing the software. After a couple more revisions, Linus released version 0.95 in March 1992 as a way of reflecting his expectation that the system was prepared for an 'official' release real soon.

About one year and a half later (December 1993), the version was finally made it to 1.0.

Today, Linux is a total clone of Unix and has since been able to reach a user base spanning industries and continents. The people who understand it see and appreciate its use in virtually everything- from cars to smartphones, home appliances like fridges and supercomputers, this operating system is everywhere. Linux actually runs the largest part of the internet, the computers making all the scientific breakthroughs you're hearing about every other day and the world's stock exchanges.

As you appreciate its existence, don't forget that this operating system was (and still is) the most secure, reliable and hassle-free operating system available before it became the best platform to run servers, desktops and embedded systems all over the globe.

With that short history, I believe you are now ready for some information to get you up to speed on this marvelous platform.

Essential Parts Of A Linux System

Just like other Mac OS X and Windows 10, Linux is an operating system. It is made up of the following pieces:

The bootloader- This is the software that manages your computer's boot processes. Simply put, it is the splash screen that pops up and then disappears to boot into the operating system.

The kernel- If you've done some research into Linux before, you should have come across this word countless times. It refers to the piece of the whole that's referred to as *Linux*. It is the core of the system; it manages peripheral devices, CPU and memory.

Daemons- These are the background services such as scheduling, sound and printing that either start when you log into your computer or during the boot process.

Shell- You've probably also heard this word too many times as well or the *Linux command line,* which at one time scared many people away from Linux (perhaps because they thought they had to learn some mind-numbing command line structure to use the OS). The shell is the command process that lets you control your computer through commands by typing them into a text interface. Today, you can work with Linux without even touching the command line but it's important to work with it, as we are going to see shortly.

Graphical server- This is simply the sub-system that displays graphics on your monitor. It is commonly known as x or the x server.

The desktop environment- This is the actual implementation of the metaphor 'desktop' that is made of programs running on the visible surface of the operating system that you will interact with directly. You have numerous desktop environments to choose from which include gnome, enlightenment, xfce, utility and cinnamon. The desktop environment comes with a bundle of built-in applications, which include configuration tools, file managers, games and web browsers- among others.

Applications- As you may already know, desktop environments don't usually offer the full array of apps. Linux provides thousands of software titles, which you can easily access and install, which is the same case with Windows and Mac.

The above descriptions will assist you sail through the rest of the book easily. Let's now get to the part where we start using the program. The first step is choosing the distribution, as you will find out next.

Choosing Your Distribution (Distro)

Before we get started with the command line, we have to make sure you are all set up. The first thing you need to do therefore is select your distribution. Unlike Windows, Linux doesn't have a single version, and that's why we have many Linux 'distributions'.

These distributions take the kernel and combine it with other software such as a desktop environment, graphical server, web browser and many more. A distribution thus unites all these elements into one operating system that you can install and work with.

From a beginner user versions to intermediate and advanced user versions, there are versions to suit any level or need. All you have to do is download your preferred version into a USB thumb drive and install it to any number of machines you like.

Which distribution should you go for?

You need a distro that is easy to install, it needs to have great applications on it and needs to be easy to use for everyday activities. Moreover, the distro needs to be easy to tweak

13

when the need arises. It is for these reasons that I recommend the tiny core distro that weighs about 11 MB.

Introducing... tiny core!

Besides satisfying those parameters, tiny core saves so much on size and only requires you to have a wired network connection during its initial setup. The recommended amount of RAM you need here is only 128MB.

Well, you can take other considerations while choosing your distro, but it all depends on what you want to use it for. The distro we'll work with here is clearly ideal for someone who's just dipping their feet into Linux- without any considerable experience.

Also known as TCL, Tiny core Linux is a very specific distro, specially designed to be nomadic. Just like other distros, you can bring it with you and run it from a USB drive, CD or hard disk.

For this section, we're going to be using TCL as an example of how you can download and install a Linux distro.

How To Download And Install Tiny Core Linux

You can download TCL in the three different distros from this page.

http://tinycorelinux.net/downloads.html

You can take any of them and start the process. In the startup menu, you have to choose the option labelled 'core only'. Well, the core only (also known as the microcore) interface is simply a text based interface. You can just begin typing some commands here.

Let's try to download and install the TCL installation package on a hard disk.

The first command you'll use is 'tce-load –wi tc-install'. You don't have to type the 'tce' extension.

Note: In the code that follows, all the typed commands are in red, and their outputs are in black. For the first command, you'll get the following output:

```
tc@box:~$ tce-load -wi tc-install

tc-install.tcz.dep OK

fltk-1.3.tcz.dep OK

libXext.tcz.dep OK

libX11.tcz.dep OK

libxcb.tcz.dep OK

Downloading: libpng.tcz

Connecting to repo.tinycorelinux.net (89.22.99.37:80)

libpng.tcz 100% |******************************| 94208 0:00:00 ETA

libpng.tcz: OK

Downloading: libjpeg-turbo.tcz

Connecting to repo.tinycorelinux.net (89.22.99.37:80)

libjpeg-turbo.tcz 100% |******************************| 116k 0:00:00 ETA

libjpeg-turbo.tcz: OK

Downloading: libXdmcp.tcz

Connecting to repo.tinycorelinux.net (89.22.99.37:80)

libXdmcp.tcz 100% |******************************| 20480 0:00:00 ETA

libXdmcp.tcz: OK

Downloading: libXau.tcz

Connecting to repo.tinycorelinux.net (89.22.99.37:80)

libXau.tcz 100% |******************************| 12288 0:00:00 ETA

libXau.tcz: OK

Downloading: libxcb.tcz

Connecting to repo.tinycorelinux.net (89.22.99.37:80)

libxcb.tcz 100% |******************************| 208k 0:00:00 ETA
```

libxcb.tcz: OK

Downloading: libX11.tcz

Connecting to repo.tinycorelinux.net (89.22.99.37:80)

libX11.tcz 100% |*****************************| 968k 0:00:00 ETA

libX11.tcz: OK

Downloading: libXext.tcz

Connecting to repo.tinycorelinux.net (89.22.99.37:80)

libXext.tcz 100% |*****************************| 28672 0:00:00 ETA

libXext.tcz: OK

Downloading: fltk-1.3.tcz

Connecting to repo.tinycorelinux.net (89.22.99.37:80)

fltk-1.3.tcz 100% |*****************************| 440k 0:00:00 ETA

fltk-1.3.tcz: OK

Downloading: perl5.tcz

Connecting to repo.tinycorelinux.net (89.22.99.37:80)

perl5.tcz 100% |*****************************| 12892k 0:00:00 ETA

perl5.tcz: OK

Downloading: dosfstools.tcz

Connecting to repo.tinycorelinux.net (89.22.99.37:80)

dosfstools.tcz 100% |*****************************| 57344 0:00:00 ETA

dosfstools.tcz: OK

Downloading: syslinux.tcz

Connecting to repo.tinycorelinux.net (89.22.99.37:80)

syslinux.tcz 100% |*****************************| 2284k 0:00:00 ETA

syslinux.tcz: OK

Downloading: tc-install.tcz

Connecting to repo.tinycorelinux.net (89.22.99.37:80)

tc-install.tcz 100% |*******************************| 20480 0:00:00 ETA

tc-install.tcz: OK

tc@box:~$

This process will take a few minutes, but it depends on your internet link as well.

Prepare For Installation

At this point, you are now ready to install the TCL on the hard disk. You have to run the installation script as the super user- root (oh, this means you've got full control of the operating system).

tc@box:~$ sudo tc-install.sh

The script will clear the screens in between steps. The initial screen is the core installation.

Install from [R]unning OS, from booted [C]drom, or from [I]so file. (r/c/i):
c

Now press 'enter' to confirm your choice on each screen. We'll thus do that here. In the next screen, you have a choice for the type of installation; you can select the frugal installation (this refers to the installation on your hard disk) or removable media (USB drive) installation.

Select install type for **/mnt/sro/boot/core.gz Frugal**

* Use for frugal **hard drive** installations.

Note: You will be prompted for disk/partion and formatting options.

HDD * Use for **pendrives**. Your BIOS must support **USB-HDD** booting. * A single FAT partition will be made.

 Note: Requires dosfstools extension. **Warning:** This is a whole drive installation!

Zip * Use for **pendrives**. Drive will be formatted into two FAT partitions. * One small one for **USB_ZIP** boot compatibility, and used to hold Tiny Core.

 * The remaining partition will be used for backup & extensions. **Note:** Requires dosfstools and perl extensions.

 Warning: This is a whole drive installation! **Select Install type [F]rugal, [H]DD, [Z]ip. (f/h/z): f**

The 'f' in this case stands for 'frugal' installation. You're essentially building a virtual machine that works permanently, from the hard disk.

Now that you're doing a hard drive installation, you'll receive a prompt to perform disk partitioning and formatting.

First of all, you'll choose whether you're going to use the whole disk or an existing partition. For the latter, you can enter either (1-2) or (q)uit: 1. But remember that you cannot use the 'existing partition' option if you did not make any partition before installation. In this case, go with the first option: *whole disk.*

Once you select this option, you'll see another screen with all the disks in the system where you have to select the right one. They are described as sdb, sda, sr0 and so forth. Sr0 is for cd-rom, fd0 is for the floppy disk drive and sda is for the hard drive.

Select disk for core

1. fd0

2. sda

Enter selection (1 - 2) or (q)uit: 2

Your choice obviously is number 2.

The next thing is selecting whether or not you want a bootloader. If you're installing TCL on a blank disk, you will definitely need it. Since your system is empty, you have to choose yes- this is represented by 'y'.

The File Type

The next step entails selecting a file format, and your choice will depend on the type of media. If you want to install your software on a USB pen drive or something similar, you should select what is referred to a non-journaling file system such as vfat or ext2.

The ext4 and ext3 systems on the other hand have more writing cycles on the disk because they've been designed for robustness on data loss. If your USB is not designed for heavy writing operations therefore, it may malfunction. So select your file format based on your drive.

Select Formatting Option for sda

1. ext2

2. ext3

3. ext4

4. vfat

Enter selection (1 - 4) or (q)uit: 3

On the screen that follows, add the options for tce app restore directory and the display resolution:

Enter space separated boot options:

Example: vga=normal syslog showapps waitusb=5

vga=788 tce=hda1

Select 'y' on the next screen to start the installation process:

Last chance to exit before destroying all data on sda

Continue (y/..)?

When the installation process is successful, you will see something displayed on your screen that looks like this:

Writing zero's to beginning of /dev/sda

Partitioning /dev/sda

Formatting /dev/sda1

1+0 records in

1+0 records out

440 bytes (440B) copied, 0.000846 seconds, 507.9KB/s

UUID="FA02-C854"

Setting up core image on /mnt/sda1

Applying syslinux.

Installation has completed

Press Enter key to continue.

Congratulations! Your software has been installed.

Opening The Terminal

When your installation is complete, you can press either one of the following to open the terminal

- Alt+f2, and then enter gnome-terminal and tap okay or enter

- Ctrl+alt+t (Ubuntu)

- Lxterminal (Raspberry Pi)

If you had a problem cracking some elements of code in the illustrations above, the chapter below will explain to you what they mean.

Working With The Shell (Terminal)

As you already know, shell is the program that receives your commands and feeds them to the operating system to process, and then displays the output. This chapter will cover the basic commands that are used in Linux shell.

The Basic Commands

Pwd

When you first open the terminal, you'll essentially be in the user's home directory. To know which directory you're in, simply use the command 'pwd'. You will get the absolute path- that is, the path that begins from the base of the file system, also known as the root. It is essentially denoted by the forward slash '/'.

You'll thus get something like this:

/home/username

```
nayso@Alok-Aspire:~$ pwd
/home/nayso
```

ls

You can use the command 'is' when you want to know what files are in your directory (the directory you're currently in). You will be able to see all hidden files with the command 'is-a'

```
nayso@Alok-Aspire:~$ ls
Desktop              itsuserguide.desktop  reset-settings      VCD_Copy
Documents            Music                 School_Resources    Videos
Downloads            Pictures              Students_Works_10
examples.desktop     Public                Templates
GplatesProject       Qgis Projects         TuxPaint-Pictures
```

Cd

You'll use this command to go to a specific directory. For instance, if you are currently in the home folder and want to access the 'downloads' folder, you can enter 'cd downloads'. Don't forget that this command is case sensitive. You also have to type in the folder name exactly as it is. Nonetheless, there is a problem with these commands. You can imagine having a folder called raspberry pi. This means that you have to type in 'cd raspberry pi' but the shell only takes the second part (argument) of the command as a different one, this therefore means that you will receive an error stating that the directory doesn't exist. In this case therefore, you should use a backward slash:

'cd raspberry\ pi'

Typing only 'cd' and pressing enter takes you to the home directory. You can type 'cd..' to go back from a folder to the previous folder you can enter 'cd..' . That means that the two dots denote *back*.

```
nayso@Alok-Aspire:~$ cd Downloads
nayso@Alok-Aspire:~/Downloads$ cd
nayso@Alok-Aspire:~$ cd Raspberry\ Pi
nayso@Alok-Aspire:~/Raspberry Pi$ cd ..
nayso@Alok-Aspire:~$ 
```

Rmdir and mkdir

When you want to create a folder or a directory, use the command 'mkdir'. For instance, if you want to create a folder named 'diy', you will type 'mkdir diy'. Don't forget that if you want to make a directory called 'diy hacking', you'll have to type 'mkdir diy\ hacking'.

On the other hand, you will use 'rmdir' when you want to delete a directory. However, you can only use rmdir to delete an empty directory; just use 'rm' if you want to delete a directory that contains files.

```
nayso@Alok-Aspire:~/Desktop$ ls
nayso@Alok-Aspire:~/Desktop$ mkdir DIY
nayso@Alok-Aspire:~/Desktop$ ls
DIY
nayso@Alok-Aspire:~/Desktop$ rmdir DIY
nayso@Alok-Aspire:~/Desktop$ ls
nayso@Alok-Aspire:~/Desktop$ █
```

Rm

Besides what I've mentioned above, you can use 'rm-r' to only delete the directory. The 'rm' command will delete the folder as well as the files it contains.

```
nayso@Alok-Aspire:~/Desktop$ ls
newer.py  New Folder
nayso@Alok-Aspire:~/Desktop$ rm newer.py
nayso@Alok-Aspire:~/Desktop$ ls
New Folder
nayso@Alok-Aspire:~/Desktop$ rm -r New\ Folder
nayso@Alok-Aspire:~/Desktop$ ls
nayso@Alok-Aspire:~/Desktop$ █
```

Touch

This command will help you make a file, which can be anything from an empty zip file to an empty txt file. For instance:

'touch new.txt'

```
nayso@Alok-Aspire:~/Desktop$ ls
nayso@Alok-Aspire:~/Desktop$ touch new.txt
nayso@Alok-Aspire:~/Desktop$ ls
new.txt
```

Man & --help

The command 'man' will assist you know more about a command, and how to use it. It shows you the command's manual pages. For instance, 'man cd' shows the 'cd' command's manual pages.

When you type in the command name, the argument will enable it show the ways through which the command can be used- for instance 'cd -help'.

```
TOUCH(1)                      User Commands                      TOUCH(1)

NAME
       touch - change file timestamps

SYNOPSIS
       touch [OPTION]... FILE...

DESCRIPTION
       Update  the  access  and modification times of each FILE to the current
       time.

       A FILE argument that does not exist is created empty, unless -c  or  -h
       is supplied.

       A  FILE  argument  string of - is handled specially and causes touch to
       change the times of the file associated with standard output.

       Mandatory arguments to long options are  mandatory  for  short  options
       too.

       -a     change only the access time

Manual page touch(1) line 1 (press h for help or q to quit)
```

Cp

This command is used to copy files through the command line. 'cp' takes two arguments which include:

• The file's location

• Where to copy

```
nayso@Alok-Aspire:~/Desktop$ ls /home/nayso/Music/
nayso@Alok-Aspire:~/Desktop$ cp new.txt /home/nayso/Music/
nayso@Alok-Aspire:~/Desktop$ ls /home/nayso/Music/
new.txt
```

Mv

This command is used when moving commands through the command line. You can also use this command to rename a certain file. For instance, if you want the file 'text' to read 'new', you can use 'mv text new'. Just like the command 'cp', it takes the two arguments.

```
nayso@Alok-Aspire:~/Desktop$ ls
new.txt
nayso@Alok-Aspire:~/Desktop$ mv new.txt newer.txt
nayso@Alok-Aspire:~/Desktop$ ls
newer.txt
```

Locate

When you want to locate a file in the Linux system, you can use 'locate'. It is similar to the search command in Windows OS. You will find it useful when you don't know the file's actual name or where it is saved. You can use the '-i' argument with the command to ignore the case (this means it doesn't matter whether it's lowercase or uppercase).

Therefore, if you want a file that contains the word 'hello', you can enter 'locate –i hello' and you'll get a list of all files within your Linux system that contains that word. If you can remember two words, you can use the asterisk (*) to separate them. For instance assume you want to locate a file that contains the words 'this' and 'hello'. You'll use the command 'locate –i *this*hello'.

```
nayso@Alok-Aspire:~$ locate newer.txt
/home/nayso/Desktop/newer.txt
nayso@Alok-Aspire:~$ locate *DIY*Hacking*
/home/nayso/DIY Hacking
```

Now let's take a look at:

The Intermediate Commands

Echo

This command will help you move some data, usually in text form into a file. For instance, if you want to add to another that is already made or make a new text file altogether, all you have to do is simply enter:

'echo hello, my name is alok>> new.txt'.

Here, you don't need to use the backward slash to separate the spaces because you'll add two triangle brackets when you complete what you need to write.

Cat

This command is used to display file contents. You'll find it important when you want to view programs easily.

```
nayso@Alok-Aspire:~/Desktop$ echo hello, my name is alok >> new.txt
nayso@Alok-Aspire:~/Desktop$ cat new.txt
hello, my name is alok
nayso@Alok-Aspire:~/Desktop$ echo this is another line >> new.txt
nayso@Alok-Aspire:~/Desktop$ cat new.txt
hello, my name is alok
this is another line
```

Nano, jed, vi

First of all, the command 'nano' is a great text editor that denotes the colored keywords, besides being able to recognize most languages. Vi on the other hand is simpler than nano. You can make a new file or use the editor to modify a file. Let's take an example.

You want to make a file with the name 'check.txt'. You can use the 'nano check.txt' command to make it.

After editing, you can save the files with the sequence ctrl+x, and then y (yes) or n (no).

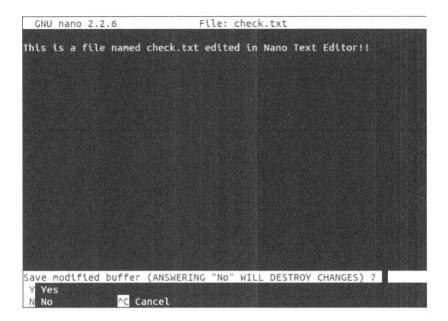

Sudo

'sudo' means 'super user do'. That means that if you want to have any command implemented with root or administrative privileges, you can invoke the 'sudo' command.

Let's take an example:

You want to edit the file 'viz. Alsa-base.conf' or any other file that requires root permission. You can use the following command:

'sudo nano alsa-base.conf'

You can use the 'sudo bash' command to enter the root command line, and then enter your user password. Another command you can use to do this is 'su', but you'll have to set a root password before that. To do that, you can enter the 'sudo passwd' command and then enter the new password.

```
nayso@Alok-Aspire:~/Desktop$ sudo passwd
[sudo] password for nayso:
Enter new UNIX password:
Retype new UNIX password:
passwd: password updated successfully
nayso@Alok-Aspire:~/Desktop$ su
Password:
root@Alok-Aspire:/home/nayso/Desktop#
```

Df

If you want to see how much disk space you have left in each of your system's partitions, you can use the 'df' command. All you have to do is type it in your command line and you'll be able to see each mounted partition and how much space is used or available in kilobytes. You can use the command 'df -m' if you want to see it displayed in megabytes.

```
root@Alok-Aspire:/home/nayso/Desktop# df -m
Filesystem     1M-blocks  Used Available Use% Mounted on
udev                 940     1       940   1% /dev
tmpfs                191     2       189   1% /run
/dev/sda5          96398 23466     68013  26% /
none                   1     0         1   0% /sys/fs/cgroup
none                   5     0         5   0% /run/lock
none                 951     1       950   1% /run/shm
none                 100     1       100   1% /run/user
```

Tar

This command is useful when you want to work with tarballs
(archives or files compressed in archives) in the command
line. You can use it to do so much; you can use it to compress
or un-compress various kinds of tar archives such as .tar.gz,
.tar and .tar.bz2. It works based on the arguments you give it.
For instance, 'tar -cvf' will create a .tar archive, -xvf will untar
a tar archive and –tvf will list the archive's contents. You can
take a look at <u>these</u> examples of tar commands to learn more.

Zip and unzip

You'll use 'zip' to compress files into a zip archive and 'unzip'
to extract them from a zip archive.

Uname

This command helps you see information about the system
your distro is running at the moment. To print out the
information about the system, you can use the 'uname-a'

command. You'll have the kernel release date, processor type, version and so on.

```
nayso@Alok-Aspire:~$ uname -a
Linux Alok-Aspire 4.4.0-22-generic #40~14.04.1-Ubuntu SMP Fri May 13 17:27:18 UT
C 2016 i686 i686 i686 GNU/Linux
```

Apt-get

'apt' comes in when you want to work with packages in Linux. 'apt-get' installs the packages. You'll require root privileges here so you'll have to use the 'sudo' command along with it. For instance, let's say you wish to install the 'jed' text editor. You'll have to type in the following:

'sudo apt-get install jed'

This is how you'll install other packages as well. You'll also want to update the repository whenever you install a brand new package- which is as simple as typing 'sudo apt-get update'. Replace the word 'update' with 'upgrade' to upgrade the distro. Moreover, the 'apt-cache search' command searches for a package.

```
nayso@Alok-Aspire:~$ sudo apt-get install jed
Reading package lists... Done
Building dependency tree
Reading state information... Done
The following extra packages will be installed:
  jed-common libslang2-modules slsh
Suggested packages:
  gpm
The following NEW packages will be installed:
  jed jed-common libslang2-modules slsh
0 upgraded, 4 newly installed, 0 to remove and 419 not upgraded.
Need to get 810 kB of archives.
After this operation, 2,992 kB of additional disk space will be used.
Do you want to continue? [Y/n]
```

Chmod

When you want to make your file more executable and change the permissions it is granted by Linux, 'chmod' is your command. You can imagine having a python code called 'numbers.py' on your computer. You'll have to run 'python numbers.py' each time you have to run it. Instead of doing that, you can simply run the file by running 'numbers.py' in the terminal. The command 'chmod +x numbers.py' will help you make the file executable in this case. You can give it root permissions with 'chmod 755 numbers.py' or, for root executable, sudo chmod +x numbers.py'.

```
nayso@Alok-Aspire:~/Desktop$ ls
numbers.py
nayso@Alok-Aspire:~/Desktop$ chmod +x numbers.py
nayso@Alok-Aspire:~/Desktop$ ls
numbers.py
```

Hostname

If you want to know the name in your network or host, simply use 'hostname'. It essentially displays your IP address and hostname. If you want to get your network IP address, simply type in 'hostname -i'.

```
nayso@Alok-Aspire:~/Desktop$ hostname
Alok-Aspire
nayso@Alok-Aspire:~/Desktop$ hostname -I
192.168.1.36
```

Ping

This command is great when it comes to checking your connection to a server. For those who are more technically inclined, it is a software utility in computer network administration that you use to test host reachability on an IP network.

Let's take a simple example: when you enter something like 'ping google.com', it checks whether it can connect to the server and come back. This round-trip time is measured and you get the full details about it. People like us however use this command for simple stuff like checking the internet connection.

In our case, if it pings the server (Google), it means your internet connection is active.

```
nayso@Alok-Aspire:~/Desktop$ ping google.com
PING google.com (172.217.26.206) 56(84) bytes of data.
64 bytes from google.com (172.217.26.206): icmp_seq=1 ttl=56 time=51.2 ms
64 bytes from google.com (172.217.26.206): icmp_seq=2 ttl=56 time=47.9 ms
64 bytes from google.com (172.217.26.206): icmp_seq=3 ttl=56 time=48.9 ms
^C
--- google.com ping statistics ---
3 packets transmitted, 3 received, 0% packet loss, time 2000ms
rtt min/avg/max/mdev = 47.959/49.388/51.299/1.417 ms
```

Let's Try Out Something

It is highly likely you are sitting in front of your computer screen; your terminal window is open and you're wondering.... "so, what should I do now?" the terminal window in front of you contains shell, which enables you to use commands like the ones we've just gone through to interact with your computer, thus store or retrieve data, process information and many other simple or even overly complex tasks.

Your first activity is to try this out: type some commands using your keyboard like 'cal', 'Is', 'pwd' or 'date' and then tap the 'enter' key.

By typing those commands, you've just interacted with your computer to look up a calendar (with 'cal'), retrieve a list of all directories and files in your computer (with 'Is'), check your present working directory's location (with 'pwd') and retrieved the date and time (with 'date').

Scripting

Now picture yourself executing all the commands above on a daily basis. Every day, you have to execute all these commands and store the observed information without fail. It will not take long before you become extremely tired of this task that is clearly destined for failure. The obvious solution here is looking for a way to execute all the commands together.

Scripting comes in here as your solution and salvation.

```
linuxconfig.org:~$ vi task.sh
linuxconfig.org:~$ chmod +x task.sh
linuxconfig.org:~$ ./task.sh                    Fri 31 Mar
12:56:09 AEDT 2017                    March 2017
Su Mo Tu We Th Fr Sa                           1  2  3  4
5  6  7  8  9 10 11              12 13 14 15 16 17 18
19 20 21 22 23 24 25                  26 27 28 29 30
31
/home/linuxconfig                     hello-world.sh
task.sh                    linuxconfig.org:~$
```

You can clearly see from the image above that with scripting, you can be able to automate any shell interaction and script it. Scripting is therefore a function that enables commands to be executed automatically instead of being executed interactively one by one.

How About Bash?

Bash is a term you'll get countless times in this book. Bash is the default interpreter on most Linux or GNU systems; we've been using it without even knowing it! This is the reason why the last shell script works without you defining bash as the interpreter. You can execute the command 'echo $SHELL' to see your default interpreter though.

Well, we have a couple of other shell interpreters in use currently such as C shell and Korn shell. Therefore, it is always good practice to explicitly define the shell interpreter that's supposed to be used to interpret the content of the script. Therefore, if you want to define the interpreter of your script as 'bash', start by locating a full path to the specific executable binary with the command 'which', have the shebang '#!' as its prefix and let it be the first line of your script. We definitely have many other ways of defining shell interpreter but this is a good place to start.

```
/bin/bash                           linuxconfig.org:~$ vi
task.sh                        linuxconfig.org:~$ ./task.sh
Fri 31 Mar 14:24:24 AEDT 2017                      March
2017                        Su Mo Tu We Th Fr Sa
1  2  3  4                       5  6  7  8  9 10 11
12 13 14 15 16 17 18               19 20 21 22 23 24
25                          26 27 28 29 30 31
/home/linuxconfig                        hello-world.sh
task.sh                         linuxconfig.org:~$
```

The Execution Of Scripts

Let's now talk about another way of running scripts in bash. One very simplistic view of bash is that it is merely a text file that contains instructions that have to be executed from top to bottom, in order. The way instructions are interpreted solely depends on defined shebang or the particular way the script is executed. Let's take a simple example:

```
linuxconfig.org:~$ echo date > date.sh       linuxconfig.org:~$ cat
date.sh  date                                 linuxconfig.org:~$ ./date.sh
bash: ./date.sh: Permission denied            linuxconfig.org:~$ bash
date.sh                                        Thu 20 Jul 11:46:30 AEST 2017
linuxconfig.org:~$ vi date.sh                 linuxconfig.org:~$ chmod
+x date.sh                                    linuxconfig.org:~$ ./date.sh
Thu 20 Jul 11:46:49 AEST 2017                 linuxconfig.org:~$
```

Alternatively, you can execute bash scripts by calling the bash interpreter explicitly- for instance '$ bash date.sh', therefore executing the script without having to make the shell executable or even directly declaring shebang inside a shell script. When you explicitly call bash executable binary, the content of the file 'date.sh' is usually loaded after which it is interpreted as what's referred to as Bash Shell Script.

The relative and absolute path

Finally, before we get into a more exciting part of this book, let's have a brief look into shell navigation and the difference between absolute and relative file path.

Perhaps the best way to look at absolute and relative file paths is visualizing GNU or Linux file systems as a building with many stories. The root entrance door to the building is the root directory; it is indicated by the symbol '/'and it offers the entry to the whole building or file system in this case, thus giving access to all the levels or rooms (the directories) and people (the files).

To get to the first room on the third floor/level, you would first have to enter the main door '/' and then go to the third level 'level3/', and from there, enter 'room1'. Therefore, the specific path to this room inside a building is '/level3/room1'. Once you are here, if you wish to go to the second room on level 3, you first have to leave your current location, which is room 1 by typing '../' and then entering the name of that room, that is 'room2'.

With that, we just took a relative path to the second room; in this case, that is '../room2'. We already were on level 3 already, so there was no need to leave the whole building and

take   absolute   path   through   the   main   entrance
'/level3/room2'.

Luckily, Linux has a simple compass tool to assist us navigate
throughout the file system; that is in the form of the
command 'pwd'. When this command is executed, it always
prints your current location. The example below uses the
commands 'cd' and 'pwd' to navigate the Linux file system
with both absolute and relative paths.

```
linuxconfig.org:~$ cd /
linuxconfig.org:/$ pwd                              /
linuxconfig.org:/$ cd home/
linuxconfig.org:/home$ pwd
/home
linuxconfig.org:/home$ cd ..
linuxconfig.org:/$ pwd                              /
linuxconfig.org:/$ ls                               bin  etc
initrd.img.old lib64    media proc sbin tmp vmlinuz      boot
home     lib       libx32    mnt  root srv usr vmlinuz.old
dev  initrd.img lib32     lost+found opt  run sys var
linuxconfig.org:/$ cd /etc/
linuxconfig.org:/etc$ cd ../home/linuxconfig/
linuxconfig.org:~$ pwd
/home/linuxconfig
linuxconfig.org:~$ cd -                             /etc
linuxconfig.org:/etc$ pwd                           /etc
linuxconfig.org:/etc$ cd -
/home/linuxconfig
linuxconfig.org:~$ pwd
/home/linuxconfig
linuxconfig.org:~$ cd ../../
linuxconfig.org:/$ pwd                              /
linuxconfig.org:/$ cd
linuxconfig.org:~$ pwd
/home/linuxconfig
linuxconfig.org:~$
```

Side note

You don't have to despair if you have not exactly understood what we've discussed in this section, as you probably thought you would; all this will be echoed multiple times in the subsequent chapters of this book.

That said, let's create some basic shell scripts using the command line.

How To Create Basic Scripts

As we've seen when you begin learning the command line interface, you generally explore it interactively. That means that you enter one command at a time so that you see the results of each one.

As we begin this section, you can first take a look at this gif (http://bit.ly/2linux3) which explores a Shakespearean plays' directory using the command line; it counts the number of words and the frequency or how many times the term 'murder' appears in all the plays of Shakespeare.

It's totally fine to use the command-line interface in this interactive manner when you're trying out things but as you may likely notice, typing is one of those activities that are prone to errors. For tasks that are more complex i.e. tasks that you want to repeat, you don't want to retype the code right from the beginning, but make a self-contained shell script that's possible to run as a one-liner.

Your First Shell Script

We'll begin with something simple. Create a junk directory somewhere, like /tmp/my-playground. Your actual workspace doesn't have to be littered with test code.

A shell script is simply a text file that has to make sense. To create one, we'll use the nano text editor.

Nano?

Nano is a text editor. It comes preinstalled in nearly all Linux distros. New users prefer it mainly because of its simplicity, which stands out when compared to other command line text editors like emacs and vi/vim. It basically contains many other useful features like line numbering, syntax coloring and easy search (among others).

Let's continue.

We'll create a shell script called hello.sh. Just follow the following steps:

Type 'nano hello.sh' and run

Nano will open and give you a blank file to work in. Now enter the following shell command.

Echo 'hello world'

On your keyboard, press ctrl +x to exit the editor. When asked whether you want to save the file, press yes (y).

Nano will then confirm whether you want to save the file. Press enter to confirm the action.

Now run the script 'hello. sh' with the following command:

Bash hello.sh

When you look at it as a gif, the steps look something like this.

http://bit.ly/2piclinux

Therefore, 'hello.sh' is not particularly exciting, but at least it catches the essence of what you want to do, which is to wrap up a series of commands into a file, that is, a script, so that you can re-run the script as much as you'd want. That helps you remove the chance of having typographic errors that come about when you're retyping commands, and also allows you to make the script reusable in various contexts.

Having Arguments In A Re-Usable Shell Script

Let's now try making 'hello. sh' a bit complicated. Now instead of repeating hello world, you'll create the script in such a way that it says 'hello' to a certain value- for instance, a person's name. That will make the script seem a bit better. You can use it like so:

```
bash hello.sh Dan

HELLO DAN
```

The gif is as <u>follows</u>.

<u>http://bit.ly/2linux5</u>

First off, you customize 'hello world' by adding a variable in the place of 'world'. Try to do that from the command line interactively:

yourname=Dan

echo "Hello $yourname"

The output is:

Hello Dan

Therefore, the question here is, how do you get the script 'hello.sh' to read in our argument (which is a person's name in this case) that you pass into it?

```
bash hello.sh George
```

You do that through a special bash variable. The first, second and third arguments you passed from the command line into the script are denoted by the variables which include $1, $2, $3. In the example above therefore, the name George will be kept in the variable $1 as 'hello.sh' starts running.

Just reopen 'hello.sh' and change your code to the following

```
$yourname=$1
echo "Hello $yourname"
```

After saving the changes, now run the following to see the output.

```
bash hello.sh Mary
```

If you desire to have the output returned in all caps, simply modify 'hello.sh' in the following manner, making sure to pipe the output through 'tr' in order to replace all the lowercase letters with those in the uppercase.

```
$yourname=$1

echo "Hello $yourname" | tr '[[:lower:]]' '[[:upper:]]'
```

Now if you have a desire to be concise, you may find that '$yourname' variable is not really necessary. The code will be simplified like so:

```
echo "Hello $1" | tr '[[:lower:]]' '[[:upper:]]'
```

Now slow down my friend. If you are able to create a script, you can execute like so:

```
bash hello.sh
```

...then congratulations, you've learned an important concept. You've just learned how programmers stuff complicated things into a 'container' that can be run into one line. Before we start making some decisions, let's see how we can use a feature known as variables to refer to data, which includes commands' output or results.

Bash Variables And Command Substitution

In programming, there is one important aspect you have to note: that is the ability to use a label or a name to refer to another quantity, which includes a command, or a value. It is known as *variables*.

Variables are symbolic names for chunks of memory to which values can be assigned and its contents read and manipulated. At the very least, these 'symbolic names' helps make code more readable to us.

Nonetheless, variables essentially become more practical or useable in more advanced programming where you'll find situations where the actual values are not known- that is, before a program is executed. A variable is therefore more like a placeholder that is solved upon the actual execution time.

Let's take an example:

Assume 'websites. txt' has a list of website addresses. The routine below reads every line (through 'cat' which is really not best practice- but it will do for now) into a 'for loop', which in turn downloads all the URLs (please find details about for loops in the next chapter).

```
for url in $(cat websites.txt); do
  curl $url > megapage.html
done
```

Before you start getting confused, let me take you through a little introduction of the basic usage and syntax of variables.

Setting A Variable

The command below assigns 'Hello world' to 'var_a' variable and '42' to 'another_var'

```
user@host:~$ var_a="Hello World"
user@host:~$ another_var=42
```

Unlike most languages that you'll find today, bash is quite picky about the variable setting syntax. More specifically, it doesn't allow any whitespace between the name of the variable, the equal sign and the value.

These three examples would easily trigger an error from Bash:

```
var_a= "Hello World"
var_a = "Hello World"
var_a ="Hello World"
```

Referencing The Variable's Value

Each time bash comes across this sign: '$', after which there is a word in a double-quoted string or inside a command, it will try to replace that particular token with the named variable's value. Sometimes, that is referred to as parameter substitution or expanding the variable.

```
user@host:~$ var_a="Hello World"
user@host:~$ another_var=42
user@host:~$ echo $var_a
Hello World
user@host:~$ echo $another_var
42
user@host:~$ echo $var_a$another_var
Hello World42
```

When De-Referencing Is Not Done

In the instance the sign '$' is not preceding the name of a variable, or the variable reference is inside single quotes, bash interprets the string literally like so:

```
user@host:~$ var_a="Hello World"
user@host:~$ another_var=42
user@host:~$ echo var_a
var_a
user@host:~$ echo '$another_var'
$another_var
user@host:~$ echo "$var_a$another_var"
Hello World42
user@host:~$ echo '$var_a$another_var'
$var_a$another_var
```

Concatenating Strings

You will find variables very useful when it comes to text-patterns that you'll use repeatedly:

```
user@host:~$ wh_domain='http://www.whitehouse.gov'
user@host:~$ wh_path='/briefing-room/press-briefings?page='
user@host:~$ wh_base_url="$wh_domain$wh_path"
user@host:~$ curl -so 10.html "$wh_base_url=10"
user@host:~$ curl -so 20.html "$wh_base_url=20"
user@host:~$ curl -so 30.html "$wh_base_url=30"
```

If the name of your variable is butting up against some literal alphanumeric character, this verbose form that involves curly braces will come in handy to reference the value of a variable:

```
user@host:~$ BASE_BOT='R2'
user@host:~$ echo "$BASE_BOTD2"
# nothing gets printed, because $BASE_BOTD2 is interpreted
# as a variable named BASE_BOTD2, which has not been set
user@host:~$ echo "${BASE_BOT}D2"
R2D2
```

The Valid Names For Variables

A variable name can have underscores and a sequence of alphanumeric characters. All the variables you create, as the user should begin with either an underscore or an alphabetical letter; not a number.

Here are some valid names for variables:

hey
x9
GRATUITOUSLY_LONG_NAME
_secret

When you write functions and scripts, in which arguments are passed in for processing, the arguments will automatically be passed 'int' variables named numerically-for instance, $2 and $3. A good example would be:

bash my_script.sh Hello 42 World

Commands will use $1 within 'my_script . sh' in reference of 'Hello', '$2' to '42' and '$3' for 'world'.

Take a look at the variable reference below:

'$0'

It will expand to the present name of the script- for instance, 'my_script . sh

Command Substitution

A command standard's output can be encapsulated, pretty much the same way a value can be stored in a value, before then being expanded by the shell. This concept is known as command substitution.

Going by the bash documentation, command substitution basically allows a command's output to replace the command itself. In bash, the expansion is done by executing command and having the command substitution take the place of the command's standard output, with all the trailing newlines erased. The embedded newlines don't get erased, but during word splitting, they may be deleted.

Let's take an example:

Consider the command 'seq'. It will print a sequence of numbers beginning from the first argument to the second one as follows:

user@host~:$ seq 1 5

1

2

3

4

5

Command substitution can help you encapsulate the 'seq 1 5' result into a variable. This is through enclosing the command with $(and), and passing it as an argument to a different command.

user@host~:$ echo $(seq 1 5)

1 2 3 4 5

Or, to create 5 new directories:

user@host~:$ mkdir $(seq 1 5)

Variables And Command Expansion

Sometimes a command is replaced by its standard output; the output, which, presumably, is just text, can therefore be assigned to a variable just like any other value:

```
user@host~:$ a=$(echo 'hello' | tr '[:lower:]' '[:upper:]')
user@host~:$ b=$(echo 'WORLD' | tr '[:upper:]' '[:lower:]')
user@host~:$ echo "$a, $b"
HELLO, world
```

When Newlines Are Omitted

I earlier noted something from the bash documentation.

Let me give you a deeper version of that excerpt:

With command substitution, the command output is able to replace the command itself. Bash executes the command and replaces command substitution with the command's standard output- that is how it performs the expansion. Note that at the same time, any trailing newlines are deleted. The embedded newlines don't get removed, but as I mentioned earlier, they may be deleted during the process of word splitting.

In case you're wondering what that means, consider 'seq 1 5' being called as it normally would, and then, through command substitution, and take note of how the formatting changes.

```
user@host:~$ seq 1 5
1
2
3
4
5
user@host:~$ echo $(seq 1 5)
1 2 3 4 5
```

But why are the newlines getting removed during the command expansion? This is something we'll experience later; it's all about the way bash essentially interprets space and newline characters during the expansion. In any case, you may want to note the behavior for now, because it may be new to you if you're particularly coming from a different programming language.

Arithmetic Expansion

If you want to do some basic calculations, you could go ahead to enclose an expression within '$(())' like so:

```
user@host:~$ echo "42 - 10 is...$(( 42 - 10))"
42 - 10 is...32
```

You can check the <u>bash documentation</u> for all the arithmetic operators. Usually, most people find math a bit clunky when it's at the command line, so I won't bore you with too much of it.

The Utility 'bc'

<u>The 'bc' is important and useful if you want to perform more advanced math calculations from the command line. Bc reads in from 'stdout' and evaluates the expression as follows:</u>

```
user@host:~$ echo "9.45 / 2.327" | bc
4
user@host:~$ echo "9.45 / 2.327" | bc -l
4.06102277610657498925
```

Word-Splitting In The Wild

This is a short section on how bash deals with space characters when it performs an expansion.

Given that many people are used to copying and pasting code directly from the internet, it's worth knowing the various ways you could harm yourself without knowing it. This is due to the manner in which bash handles usually treats newline characters and spaces.

The Internal Field Separator

The Internal field separator 'IFS' is used by bash to split strings into distinct words. You can think of it as the way excel splits a comma-separated-values (CSV) text file into spreadsheets; according to it, commas separate the columns.

We'll assume that IFS is set to something arbitrary, such as Z. When a variable is expanded by bash, which contains a 'Z', that value's variable will be split into distinct words (in that case, the literal Z disappears):

```
user@host:~$ IFS=Z
user@host:~$ story="The man named Zorro r
user@host:~$ echo '>>' $story '<<'
>> The man named  orro rides a  ebra <<
```

The IFS variable is by default set to three characters, which include space, tab and newline. If you echo '$IFS', you will not be able to see anything since, obviously, it wouldn't be possible to see a space character without any visible characters. So what is the upshot? Simple, you may see snippets of code online in which the variable 'IFS' is changed to $ '\n' (this stands for 'newline character') or something similar.

Imagine having a text file that has a set of lines of text, which, for instance, may refer to filenames as follows:

rough draft.tx
draft 1.txt
draft 2.txt
final draft.txt

When each line of the file is read, the IFS' default value (which definitely includes a space character), causes bash to treat the file: 'rough draft . txt' as a double or two files which are 'rough' and 'draft . txt', this is because splitting words uses the space character.

When IFS is set to the newline character, the 'rough draft . txt' becomes treated as one filename.

As you will notice, this concept makes a lot of sense when it actually comes to operating on each and every line and reading text files. It might not be possible to understand this fully but you it is important you become aware of it, at least just in case you're used to copy-pasting code from the internet haphazardly.

How Bad Can Unquoted Variables Be?

In a nice, ideal world, we all would keep our string values short and devoid of space or newlines, and any other special characters. In such a world, the unquoted variable reference below would work perfectly:

```
user@host:~$ file_to_kill='whatsup.txt'
usr@host:~$ rm $file_to_kill  # delete the file named
whatsup.txt
```

However, when we start adding special characters to filenames, like spaces and expanding variables without using double quotes, it can be detrimental. In the example below, I want the file by the name 'junk final.docx' deleted:

```
user@host:~$ file_to_kill='Junk Final.docx'
```

Unanticipated word-splitting

Nonetheless, when referenced without double quotes, bash perceives 'file_to_kill' as one that has two separate values that include 'junk' and 'final.docx' below:

68

```
user@host:~$ file_to_kill='Junk Final.docx'
user@host:~$ rm $file_to_kill
rm: cannot remove 'Junk': No such file or directory
rm: cannot remove 'Final.docx': No such file or directory
```

Unanticipated special characters

You might think, "but there's no harm done" because those files did not even exist in the first place. That's fine, but what would happen if someone placed an asterisk into a filename? You do know what happens when someone does 'grep *' and 'rm *' don't you? The star acts like a hungry bear, grabbing all the files.

```
user@host:~$ file_to_kill='Junk * Final.docx'
user@host:~$ rm $file_to_kill
```

Given that 'junk' and 'final.docx' are nonexistent, you'll be able to see the previous errors. However, in between those tried deletions, 'rm' runs on the asterisk. So, just say goodbye to all the files in that directory.

You do see how 'rm "$filename" only affects the file named '* LOL BYE FILES'. Therefore, the main takeaway here is *always use double quotes in your variable references as often as you can.*

Here's a little more info that you deserve...

You might be thinking 'who in the world would place a star character in their filename?' For one, we do have folks who enjoy star-shaped symbols; also, we have malicious hackers and annoying prank-stars who wouldn't mind using a star character. Note that variables are usually not just assigned as a result of human typing; as you already know, at times, the result of commands are stored in a variable. In the instance raw data is being processed by such commands, it is possible that that kind of data does contain special characters that can damage certain bash programs.

You always have to keep it in mind the dangers of just pasting in code that seems safe. The syntax and behavior of bash in handling strings is quite difficult to understand, which is why developers turn to other languages to go about more complex applications.

From all that reading, I think you need a little break. Take a time-out by going through some basic aspects of bash that will help you in the next chapter, which are numeric and string comparisons.

Breather: Numeric And String Comparisons

In this tiny section, we're going to go through a few fundamentals of numeric and string comparisons in bash shell. With comparisons, you can compare strings (which is words and sentences) or numbers that are integers whether they are raw or as variables. Look at the table below that lists rudimentary comparison operators for strings and numbers:

Description	Numeric Comparison	String Comparison
Shell comparison example:	*[100 -eq 50]; echo $?*	*["GNU" = "UNIX"]; echo $?*
less than	-lt	<
greater than	-gt	>
equal	-eq	=
not equal	-ne	!=
less or equal	-le	N/A
greater or equal	-ge	N/A

When you review the table above, let's now assume you'd like to make a comparison between numeric values such as two integers: 1 and 2. The example below will first and foremost define two variables to hold our integer values; these are $a and $b.

After that, we are going to use square brackets and numeric comparison operators to do the actual evaluation. With the 'echo $' command, we are going to check the previously executed evaluation's return value. Note that for every evaluation, there can only be two possible outcomes, which is *true* or *false*. If the return value happens to be equal to zero, it means the comparison evaluation is true. Nonetheless, the evaluation will result as false in the instance the return value is equal to 1.

```
linuxconfig.org:~$ a=1
linuxconfig.org:~$ b=2
linuxconfig.org:~$ [ $a -lt $b ]
linuxconfig.org:~$ echo $?                    0
linuxconfig.org:~$ [ $a -gt $b ]
linuxconfig.org:~$ echo $?                    1
linuxconfig.org:~$ [ $a -eq $b ]
linuxconfig.org:~$ echo $?                    1
linuxconfig.org:~$ [ $a -ne $b ]
linuxconfig.org:~$ echo $?                    0
linuxconfig.org:~$
```

With string comparison operators, you can also be able to compare strings pretty much the same way you would when comparing numeric values. Take the following example:

```
linuxconfig.org:~$ [ "apples" = "oranges" ]
linuxconfig.org:~$ echo $?                        1
linuxconfig.org:~$ str1="apples"
linuxconfig.org:~$ str2="oranges"
linuxconfig.org:~$ [ $str1 = $str2 ]
linuxconfig.org:~$ echo $?                        1
linuxconfig.org:~$
```

Now if the knowledge above were to be translated to a simple bash shell script, the script would look something like what is shown below. With the string comparison operator '=', you are able to compare two distinct strings to be able to see whether they are equal.

Likewise, we compare two integers with the numeric comparison operator so that we know whether they are equal in value. Don't forget that 0 signals 'true', and 1 is an indication of 'false':

```
#!/bin/bash

string_a="UNIX"
string_b="GNU"

echo "Are $string_a and $string_b strings equal?"
[ $string_a = $string_b ]
echo $?

num_a=100
num_b=100

echo "Is $num_a equal to $num_b ?"
[ $num_a -eq $num_b ]
echo $?
```

Now save the script above as something like 'comparison.sh' file and make it executable; now execute as follows:

```
$ chmod +x compare.sh

$ ./compare.sh
```

Are UNIX and GNU strings equal?

1

Is 100 equal to 100 ?

0

When you use numeric comparison operators to compare strings with integers, it will often result in this error: 'integer expression expected'. When you're comparing values, you will want to use the 'echo' command to first confirm that your variables are holding expected values before you use them in the comparison operation.

Well, besides having an educational value, the script above doesn't really serve any other purpose. When you learn about conditional statements such as if/else in the next chapter, comparison operators will make a lot more sense. This section is therefore applied in conditional statements, which is where we'll put comparison operators to better use.

It's now time you learnt how to make decisions in your scripts. Keep reading.

Bash "If Statements"

You'll now learn how to automate tasks in your bash scripts using bash if statements. "If statements" essentially allow you to decide whether you should run a piece of code (or not) based on conditions that you may set.

Basic "If Statements"

According to a basic if statement, if a certain test is true, you should then do a certain set of actions. If it is not true, you should not. It follows this format:

```
if [ <some test> ]
then
<commands>
fi
```

Anything that between then and the 'if backwards' denoted by 'fi' is automatically executed if the test (which is between the square brackets) is true. Take a look at this example:

```
1.  #!/bin/bash
2.  # Basic if statement
3.
4.  if [ $1 -gt 100 ]
5.  then
6.  echo Hey that\'s a large number.
7.  pwd
8.  fi
9.
10.  date
```

Just to break it down for you-

We're trying to see whether the first command line argument is more than 100 (in line 4).

In the sixth and seventh line, you can see that it will only run if the test (on the fourth line) returns true. Note you can have whatever number of commands here as you want.

In the sixth line, you can see the backslash before the single quote is required. The single quote has a special meaning for bash and we don't need that special meaning. With the backslash, you are able to escape the special meaning to take it back to a plain single quote.

fi (in the eighth line) marks the end of the if statements. Any command after this will run as normal.

Since this command (in line 10) is outside the if statement, it will run regardless of the if statement's outcome

1. ./if_example.sh 15
2. Mon 14 Jan 0:26:25 2019
3. ./if_example.sh 150
4. Hey that's a large number.
5. /home/ryan/bin
6. Mon 14 Jan 0:26:25 2019
7.

It's always important to test scripts with input that can cover the different possible scenarios.

The Test

These square brackets '[]' that you can see in the 'if' statements reference the 'test' command. That means that all the operators that test allows can be used here too. You can look at some of the most common possible operators below:

Operator	Description
! EXPRESSION	The EXPRESSION is false.
-n STRING	The length of STRING is greater than zero.
-z STRING	The lengh of STRING is zero (ie it is empty).
STRING1 = STRING2	STRING1 is equal to STRING2
STRING1 != STRING2	STRING1 is not equal to STRING2
INTEGER1 -eq INTEGER2	INTEGER1 is numerically equal to INTEGER2
INTEGER1 -gt INTEGER2	INTEGER1 is numerically greater than INTEGER2
INTEGER1 -lt INTEGER2	INTEGER1 is numerically less than INTEGER2
-d FILE	FILE exists and is a directory.
-e FILE	FILE exists.
-r FILE	FILE exists and the read permission is granted.
-s FILE	FILE exists and it's size is greater than zero (ie. it is not empty).
-w FILE	FILE exists and the write permission is granted.
-x FILE	FILE exists and the execute permission is granted.

There are a few things you need to note though:

The sign '=' is a bit different from −eq. Therefore [001 = 1] returns false the same way '=' does a string comparison, and −eq does numerical comparisons which means [001-eq 1] returns true.

The 'file' above refers to a path. A path may refer to a directory or file.

Since [] is simply a reference to the 'test' command, you may experiment then trouble shoot on the command line with test to ensure your understanding of its behavior is right.

```
1.  test 001 = 1
2.  echo $?
3.  1
4.  test 001 -eq 1
5.  echo $?
6.  0
7.  touch myfile
8.  test -s myfile
9.  echo $?
10.  1
11. ls /etc > myfile
12. test -s myfile
13. echo $?
14. 0
15.
```

Let me break that down a bit for you.

Line 1: do a comparison based comparison. Given that test doesn't print the result, you instead have to check its exit status; that is in the line that follows.

Line 2: the '$' variable holds the exit status of the command that was previously run (that is, the test). Zero denotes true or success whereas 1 denotes false or failure.

Line 4: you're now doing a numerical comparison

Line 7: a new blank file known as 'myfile' is created- this is assuming that it doesn't exist already.

Line 8: is 'myfile' greater than zero in terms of size?

Line 11: pass on some content into 'myfile' to have its size more than zero.

Line 12: retest the size of the file. It's true this time round.

Indenting

Indenting is the manner in which you *organize* and document source code.

As you may notice, we indented the commands (in the 'if' statements above) that run when the statement was true. This is known as indenting and is important when it comes to writing clean code. Indenting helps improve your code's readability and minimizes the chances of making silly mistakes.

It's important to note that there are no indentation rules in bash, which means that you may (or may not indent) and your scripts will run the exact same way.

Nonetheless, particularly as your scripts become bigger, you will find it more difficult to see your scripts' structure, which makes it critical to always have your code indented.

Nested If Statements

While we're still on the topic of indenting, this is one great example showing how it can make life simple for you. Your script may have many 'if' statements as there can be; you can also have an "if" statement within another "statement".

For instance, you may want to analyze the number given on the command line as follows:

```
1.  #!/bin/bash
2.  # Nested if statements
3.
4.  if [ $1 -gt 100 ]
5.  then
6.  echo Hey that\'s a large number.
7.
8.  if (( $1 % 2 == 0 ))
9.  then
10.   echo And is also an even number.
11. fi
12.fi
```

Let's break that down:

In the fourth line, it's clear that you only perform the following if the first command line argument is more than 100.

In the eighth line, we see a little variation on the 'if' statement. If you want to check any expression, you may utilize the double brackets.

In the tenth line, both 'if' statements have to be true for it to get run.

Tip

Generally, although you can easily nest as many if statements, as you possibly can and want to, it is important to consider reorganizing your logic if you want to nest more than three levels deep.

If Else

You'd agree with me that there are times when you would want to perform a particular action if a statement is true, and definitely another set of actions if it is false. You can fit this in with the 'else' mechanism.

Take a look:

```
if [ <some test> ]
then
<commands>
else
<other commands>
fi
```

You could now read from with ease especially if it has been delivered as a command line argument, 'else' which is read from "stdin" as illustrated below.

Note: Stdin (standard input) is an input stream where data is sent to a program and read by the program. This will be discussed more shortly.

1. #!/bin/bash
2. # else example
3.
4. if [$# -eq 1]
5. then
6. nl $1
7. else
8. nl /dev/stdin
9. fi

If Elif Else

We also have times when we have a series of conditions that may lead to different paths.

Take a look:

```
if [ <some test> ]


then
<commands>
elif [ <some test> ]
then
<different commands>
else
<other commands>
fi
```

This may be the case in this example:

You are 18 years or above, so you may go to a party; if you are not, but have an okay from your guardians, you may go but have to be back by midnight. Otherwise, you can't attend the party.

This is how it looks:

```
1.  #!/bin/bash
2.  # elif statements
3.
4.  if [ $1 -ge 18 ]
5.  then
6.  echo You may go to the party.
7.  elif [ $2 == 'yes' ]
8.  then
9.  echo You may go to the party but be back before midnight.
10.  else
11. echo You may not go to the party.
12.fi
```

You can have as many 'elif' branches as you want; the final else is also optional.

Boolean Operators

Now, what if you only want to do something if multiple conditions are met? Indeed, there are times when you'll want to perform the action if one or more conditions are met. This is where Boolean operators come in (to accommodate these).

They include:

- And (&&)

- Or (||)

As an example, consider that you want to perform an operation if your file is both readable and its size is greater than zero:

```
1. #!/bin/bash
2. # and example
3.
4. if [ -r $1 ] && [ -s $1 ]
5. then
6. echo This file is useful.
7. fi
```

Perhaps you now want to do something that is a bit different if the user is either Andy or Bob:

```
1. #!/bin/bash
2. # or example
3.
4. if [ $USER == 'bob' ] || [ $USER == 'andy' ]
5. then
6. ls -alh
7. else
8. ls
9. fi
```

Case Statements

You may also want to take a different path based upon a variable corresponding to series of patterns. You can obviously use a series of 'elif' and 'if' statements but that would soon become unwieldy. Luckily, we can use a 'case' statement to make things cleaner.

Take a look at the following examples to understand what I'm talking about:

```
case <variable> in
<pattern 1>)
<commands>
;;
<pattern 2>)
<other commands>
;;
esac
```

Here's a more basic example:

```
1.  #!/bin/bash
2.  # case example
3.
4.  case $1 in
5.  start)
6.  echo starting
7.  ;;
8.  stop)
9.  echo stoping
10.  ;;
11. restart)
12. echo restarting
13. ;;
14. *)
15. echo don\'t know
16. ;;
17. esac
```

Now let me break that down for you:

In the fourth line, we see that the line starts the mechanism 'case'.

In the fifth line, 'start' is equal to $1; you then perform the actions that follow. ')' denotes the end of that pattern.

In the seventh line, the end of this set of statements is identified with a double semi-colon (;;). The next case to consider follows this.

In the fourteenth line, you have to note that the test for each case is a pattern. '*' denotes any number of any character. It essentially is a catch-all in the instance no other cases match. It is often used even though it is not necessary.

In the last line, we see esac. It is 'case backwards'; it shows you that you are at the end of the case statement. All other statements after this one are executed normally.

1. ./case.sh start
2. starting
3. ./case.sh restart
4. restarting
5. ./case.sh blah
6. don't know
7.

Let's now take a look at one slightly complex case where the use of patterns is slightly more.

```
1.  #!/bin/bash
2.  # Print a message about disk useage.
3.
4.  space_free=$( df -h | awk '{ print $5 }' | sort -n | tail -n 1 | sed
    's/%//' )
5.
6.  case $space_free in
7.  [1-5]*)
8.  echo Plenty of disk space available
9.  ;;
10.  [6-7]*)
11. echo There could be a problem in the near future
12.;;
13.8*)
14.echo Maybe we should look at clearing out old files
15.;;
16.9*)
17.echo We could have a serious problem on our hands soon
18.  ;;
19.*)
20.  echo Something is not quite right here
21.;;
22.  esac
```

Activity: make your own decisions

1. Build a Bash script that takes two numbers as command line arguments.

2. Create a script that accepts a file as a command line argument and then analyze it. For instance, you could check whether the file is writable or executable. A message should be printed if true, and another one if false.

3. Now create a script that prints a message according to the day of the week it is. For instance, 'Happy surf day' for Saturday, 'TGIF for Sunday' and so on.

Loops In Bash Scripts

Loops are one of the most important concepts in programming. Loops are particularly useful when you want to run a series of commands recurrently, until a particular condition is attained. In scripting languages like bash, loops are great when it comes to automating repetitive tasks. For instance, imagine you need to add a user to your computer system, set the user's permissions and manage his/her starting environment. You have the option of writing down the commands on a sheet and running them as you add other users or simply writing one script and passing parameters into that particular script.

In bash scripting, we basically have three loop constructs:

• For loop

• While loop

• Until loop

This section covers the basics of for loops as well as the break and continue statements (which change the flow of a loop).

The bash *for loop*

The 'for loop' simply iterates over a given list of items and executes a given set of commands. In bash, the 'for loop' takes this form:

```
for item in [LIST]
do
 [COMMANDS]
done
Copy
```

This list can be a range of numbers, strings separated by spaces, command outputs, arrays and so forth (not familiar with these terms? See the chapter on bash variables and data types).

Let's take a few examples:

Example 1: Looping over strings.

In this example, loop will iterate over each item of the list of strings and the 'element' variable will then be set to the current item.

```
for element in Hydrogen Helium Lithium Beryllium
do
  echo "Element: $element"
done
```
Copy

The loop produces this output:

```
Element: Hydrogen
Element: Helium
Element: Lithium
Element: Beryllium
```
Copy

Example 2: looping over a range of numbers

In this case, you can use the sequence expression to specify the number range or character range by defining the start and end point of the range. The sequence expression takes this form:

```
{START..END}
```
Copy

In this case, the loop will iterate through all the numbers from 0-3.

```
for i in {0..3}
do
  echo "Number: $i"
done
```
Copy

Number: 0

Number: 1

Number: 2

Number: 3

Copy

Starting from Bash 4, you can also specify an increment with ranges.

The expression takes this form:

{START..END..INCREMENT}

Copy

for i in {0..20..5}

do

  echo "Number: $i"

done

Copy

Number: 0

Number: 5

Number: 10

Number: 15

Number: 20

Copy

Example 3: Looping over array elements

You can also iterate over an array of elements with the "for loop". Below is an example in which we are defining the 'books' array and iterating over the elements of the array.

```
BOOKS=('In Search of Lost Time' 'Don Quixote' 'Ulysses'
'The Great Gatsby')

for book in "${BOOKS[@]}"; do
  echo "Book: $book"
done
Copy
Book: In Search of Lost Time
Book: Don Quixote
Book: Ulysses
Book: The Great Gatsby
```

Break And Continue Statements

You can use the break and continue statements to control the execution of the 'for loop'.

Break statement

The current loop is terminated by the break statement and passes program control to the statement following the terminated statement. When a certain condition is met, the break statement terminates the loop.

The example below shows how the loop execution is terminated when the current iterated item becomes equivalent to 'Lithium'.

```
for element in Hydrogen Helium Lithium Beryllium; do
  if [[ "$element" == 'Lithium' ]]; then
    break
  fi
  echo "Element: $element"
done

echo 'All Done!'
Copy
Element: Hydrogen
Element: Helium
All Done!
```

Continue Statement

The continue statement leaves the current loop iteration and passes program control to the subsequent loop iteration.

In the example below, the iteration is going on through a range of numbers and when the current iterated item becomes equivalent to '2' the continue statement makes the iteration go back to the start of the loop and go on with the subsequent iteration.

```
for i in {1..5}; do
  if [[ "$i" == '2' ]]; then
    continue
  fi
  echo "Number: $i"
done
Copy
Number: 1
Number: 3
Number: 4
Number: 5
Copy
```

Let's take a look at a few examples.

Renaming files containing spaces in the filename

The example below shows how you can rename all the files in your current directory with a space in its names using the bash 'for loop' by replacing space to underscore

```
for file in *\ *; do
  mv "$file" "${file// /_}"
done
Copy
```

We'll now try breaking down the code one line at a time:

Line 1: a 'for loop' is created; it iterates through a list of all the files containing a space in the name. The list is created by the expression: *\ *

Line 2: this line applies to each item on the list; it moves the file to another fresh one, thus replacing the space with an underscore '_'.

In case you're wondering, the part "${file// /_}" is simply using what is known as shell parameter expansion to have a string within a parameter in place of a pattern. Still not clear? Perhaps you need a definition:

Parameter expansion (or variable expansion) is the process of replacing syntactic structures taking the form ${parameter} and $parameter with the exact value of the parameter. Please read more on that here to learn more.

Lastly, "done" is an indication that the loop segment has come to an end.

Changing the file extension

The example below shows how you can use bash 'for loop' to rename the files that end with .jpeg in the current directory by having .jpg as the file extension in place of .jpeg

```
for file in *.jpeg; do
    mv -- "$file" "${file%.jpeg}.jpg"
done
Copy
```

As usual, let's analyze this code one line at a time:

Line 1: here, a 'for loop' is created and it iterates through a list of all files that end with .jpeg.

Line 2: this line applies to all the list items and moves the file to another one; it replaces .jpeg with .jpg. The ${file%.jpeg} uses the shell parameter expansion to have the .jpeg part deleted from the filename.

Lastly, 'done' indicates that the loop segment has come to an end.

Congratulations! You now have the basic understanding of how bash for loop is usually used to iterate through lists.

Breather: Input and Redirection Or Errors

Usually, the commands executed on Linux command line will either give out an output, require input or produce an error message. When it comes to shell scripting and working with the command line in Linux, this is one very fundamental concept. Each time you interact with the program, you execute a command, and three possible outcomes might occur. Firstly, the command might produce an expected output. Another scenario is that the command might generate an error; lastly, the command might not give out any output at all.

```
linuxconfig.org:~$ ls -l foobar
ls: cannot access 'foobar': No such file or directory
linuxconfig.org:~$ touch foobar
linuxconfig.org:~$ ls -l foobar
-rw-r--r-- 1 linuxconfig linuxconfig 0 Jul 28 10:08 foobar
linuxconfig.org:~$
```

Note that we're most interested in the output of 'Is -1 foobar' commands. Both of these commands gave out an output, which is displayed on the terminal by default. Nonetheless, both of these outputs are basically different.

The first command is trying to list the non-existing file 'foobar'. This file in turn gives out a standard error output (stderr). When the command 'touch' creates the file, the subsequent 'Is' command execution gives out standard output (stdout). Well, basically, the difference between these two outputs – that is stderr and stdout is an important concept because it lets you threat. That means that it allows you redirect each output separately. We use the notation '>' to redirect 'stdout' to a file; '2>' notation on the other hand redirects 'stderr'. '&>' redirects 'stdout' and 'stderr'. As you probably know already, the command 'cat' makes it possible to display the contents of a file.

Let's take an example:

```
linuxconfig.org:~$ ls foobar barfoo
ls: cannot access 'barfoo': No such file or directory
foobar
linuxconfig.org:~$ ls foobar barfoo > stdout.txt
ls: cannot access 'barfoo': No such file or directory
linuxconfig.org:~$ ls foobar barfoo 2> stderr.txt
foobar
linuxconfig.org:~$ ls foobar barfoo &> stdoutandstderr.txt
linuxconfig.org:~$ cat stdout.txt
foobar
linuxconfig.org:~$ cat stderr.txt
ls: cannot access 'barfoo': No such file or directory
linuxconfig.org:~$ cat stdoutandstderr.txt
ls: cannot access 'barfoo': No such file or directory
foobar
linuxconfig.org:~$
```

Tip:

If you are not sure whether your command produced 'stderr' or 'stdout', you can try redirecting its output. For instance, if you can redirect its output to a file with the notation '2>' successfully, it means your command gave out 'stderr'. On the other hand, redirecting command output with the notation '>' successfully indicates that your command did produce 'stdout'.

Back to our script. Did you notice any additional message display by the 'tar' command? This is what I'm talking about:

```
tar: Removing leading `/' from member names
```

Despite the informative nature of the message, it is relayed to the 'stderr' descriptor. In short, the message is trying to tell you that the absolute path has been removed and thus, the compressed file's extraction didn't overwrite any existing files.

I believe you now have a basic understanding of the output redirection, you can redirect the unwanted 'stderr' message with the notation '2>' to '/dev/null' in order to eliminate it. Think of '/dev/null' as some sort of data sink that throws away any data that is redirected to it. You can run 'man null' to get more information. Take a look at this 'backup.sh' version that includes the 'stderr' redirection:

```
#!/bin/bash

# This bash script is used to backup a user's home directory to
/tmp/.

user=$(whoami)
input=/home/$user
output=/tmp/${user}_home_$(date +%Y-%m-
%d_%H%M%S).tar.gz

tar -czf $output $input 2> /dev/null
echo "Backup of $input completed! Details about the output
backup file:"
ls -l $output
```

Once a new version of the 'backup.sh' script is executed, there won't be any tar 'stderr' message being displayed.

Lastly, we'll briefly cover another concept known as shell input. Besides the 'sdderr' and 'stderr' descriptors above, bash shell also has input descriptor name 'stdin'. Terminal input generally comes from a keyboard and any keystroke typed is taken as 'stdin'.

There is an alternative method which is accepting command input from a file with the notation '<'. Consider the example below where you first feed the command 'cat' from the keyboard and redirect the output to 'filel.txt'. You'll later allow the 'cat' command to read the input from 'filel.txt' with the notation:

'<':

linuxconfig.org:~$ cat > file1.txt
I am using keyboard to input text.
Cat command reads my keyboard input, converts it to stdout
which is instantly redirected to file1.txt   That is, until I press
CTRL+D
linuxconfig.org:~$ cat < file1.txt
I am using keyboard to input text.
Cat command reads my keyboard input, converts it to stdout
which is instantly redirected to file1.txt   That is, until I press
CTRL+D
linuxconfig.org:~$

Congratulations! It's time to take your skills to the next level by learning how to reuse code. Keep reading.

Functions

I'm sure you've come across this term (function) and probably wondered what it means in scripting (if not how it works and what you can do with it). This section explains all you need to learn about functions.

Functions are small scripts within a script. Think of them as tiny chunks of code, which you can call many times within your script. It really is that simple. Functions are especially useful if you have particular tasks that you want performed more than once. Instead of writing out the same code repeatedly, functions allow you to write it once and then call it all the time.

How Do You Create Functions?

Creating functions is easy; you can write one in two different formats:

```
function_name () {
<commands>
}
```
or
```
function function_name {
<commands>
}
```

There are a few things you need to note though:

- Both methods above are valid when it comes to specifying a function. They both work the same way and none of them has advantage or disadvantage over the other- so it's really just personal preference.

- When it comes to most programming languages, arguments are commonly passed to the function listed within the brackets () but in Bash, they are only there for decoration; you never place anything inside them.

- The definition of the function or the actual function itself needs to appear or be in the script before any call to the function.

Here's a simple example:

```
1. #!/bin/bash
2. # Basic function
3.
4. print_something () {
5. echo Hello I am a function
6. }
7.
8. print_something
9. print_something
```

Let's break that down a little:

In the fourth line, we've started by giving the function a name to define it.

In the fifth line, we can include as many commands as we want within the curly brackets.

In the eighth and ninth line, you will note that when a function is clearly defined, you can call it as many time as you want and it will readily execute the commands.

./function_example.sh

Hello I am a function

Hello I am a function

You should only pick the function names that are descriptive so that it is obvious what task the function is serving.

Passing Arguments

You will, more than once, want the function to process some data for you soon. In that case, you can send data to the function the same way you would pass command line arguments to a script. You have to deliver the arguments straight after the name of the function. They can be accessed as $1, $2 and so on within the function.

```
#!/bin/bash
# Passing arguments to a function

print_something () {
echo Hello $1
}

print_something Mars
print_something Jupiter

./arguments_example.sh
Hello Mars
Hello Jupiter
```

Return Values

Most programming languages incorporate a means for a function to send back data to the original location. This concept is known as return value. Bash functions, however won't allow you to do this. Nonetheless, they allow you to set a return status, which is the same as the way a command or a program exists with its exit status that shows if it was successful or not. The keyword 'return' is used to show a return status.

```
#!/bin/bash
# Setting a return status for a function

print_something () {
echo Hello $1
return 5
}

print_something Mars
print_something Jupiter
echo The previous function has a return value of $?
```

Let me break that down a bit:

In the sixth line, it's not necessary to hardcode the return status. It could be a variable.

In the eleventh line, the $? Variable contains the return status of the function or command that was run previously.

1. ./return_status_example.sh
2. Hello Mars
3. Hello Jupiter
4. The previous function has a return value of 5

Usually, the return status of 0 shows that everything was successful. A non-zero value shows that an error did occur.

If you want to return a number, say a calculation result, you should consider using the return status to achieve this. While it is not its intended purpose, it will still work. A good way to get around this is using the command substitution to have the function print the result, and only the result. Just to remind you, command substitution is the facility that enables a command to be performed or run and its result pasted back on the command line to act as an argument to another command. In other words, it refers to running a shell command and storing its output to a variable or displaying it back with the 'echo' command.

```
#!/bin/bash
# Setting a return value to a function

lines_in_file () {
cat $1 | wc -l
}


num_lines=$( lines_in_file $1 )


echo The file $1 has $num_lines lines in it.
```

As usual, let's break that down a bit:

In the fifth line, the command will print the total number of lines in the file denoted by $1.

In the eighth line, the command substitution is used to take what would ordinarily get printed to the screen and assign it to the variable named 'num_lines'

```
cat myfile.txt
Tomato
Lettuce
Capsicum
./return_hack.sh myfile.txt
The file myfile.txt has 3 lines in it.
```

You need to be careful if you choose to take this approach because failing to call the function with command substitution can lead to printing of the result to the screen. While at times that is fine (because it is what you want), it can be undesirable at other times.

Variable Scope

Scope is simply the certain parts of a script that can 'see' certain variables. A variable is, by default, visible in all parts of a script (it is global). You can also create a local variable. When you create a local variable within a function, that variable is only visible within that particular function. To achieve that, you have to use the keyword local before the variable the first time you set its value.

local var_name=<var_value>

Any expert in this field will tell you that it is good practice to use local variables inside functions to contain everything within the function and keep it that way. That ensures the variables are generally safer from being modified inadvertently by a different part of the script, which has a variable with the same name, or vice versa.

```
#!/bin/bash
# Experimenting with variable scope

var_change () {
local var1='local 1'
echo Inside function: var1 is $var1 : var2 is $var2
var1='changed again'
var2='2 changed again'
}

var1='global 1'
var2='global 2'

echo Before function call: var1 is $var1 : var2 is $var2

var_change

echo After function call: var1 is $var1 : var2 is $var2

./local_variables.sh
Before function call: var1 is global 1 : var2 is global 2
Inside function: var1 is local 1 : var2 is global 2
After function call: var1 is global 1 : var2 is 2 changed
again
```

You should always use local variables within functions. That means only using global variables as a last resort and considering whether there is a better way of doing it before you use them.

At first, scope can be difficult to get your head around. If you get confused, you can create a bash script like the one above and start tweaking it severally and changing variables here and there, as you observe the behavior when you run it.

Overriding The Command

You can give a function the same name as that of the command you would normally use on the command line. This will enable you create a wrapper- for instance, each time you call the command 'is' in your script, what you really want is 'ls -lh'. You can do this:

```
#!/bin/bash
# Create a wrapper around the command ls

ls () {
command ls -lh
}

ls
```

In the fifth line, when you have a function that contains the same name as the command, you have to place the 'command' keyword in front of the name when you want the command instead of the function -because ordinarily, the function takes precedence.

If I had not added the 'command' keyword in front of 'ls' on the fifth line, the whole thing would have ended up in an infinite loop. Even though we are within the 'ls' function, calling 'ls' would have called another instance of the 'ls' function, which would, in turn, have done the same and so forth.

Remember that it is not hard to forget the 'command' keyword, which results in an endless loop. When you come across this issue, just press the CTRL + c keys on your keyboard (at the same time) to stop the script from running. That will cancel the script or even a program each time you have a problem on the command line.

Design

It is easy to create functions in your bash scripts. Nonetheless, it does take a lot of time and experience to create good functions that can ease the whole process of writing and maintaining your scripts. Just like other aspects of life, getting to this level of complexity means having at your disposal several other ways to attain the desired outcome. Some will be better than others, thus (in this case) the need to take your time to think about the different ways you could write your code and which way is better. Sometimes the better option is using as few lines of code as possible; sometimes it's all about what can be modified with greatest ease in future to meet changing requirements. Sometimes it is better to take an approach that is least prone to errors. If you have a task that needs to be done severally, it is a great candidate to place inside a function.

Indeed, sometimes it's great to place ancillary tasks inside functions as well so that they are logically detached from the main section of the script. One good example is validating input- for instance, ensuring a specified file is present and is readable. A function is generally most reusable when it processes one task, and that task only. Rather than having a huge function, you should consider breaking it up into a number of functions and reducing that task. However, you have to find a good balance. If you find the functions too large and taking on too much processing, it means you are not getting the full benefit. Again, if you divide it up into too many functions, it means your code will possibly swell easily and become awkward. With experience though, you'll definitely find that sweet spot at the center.

User Interface

This section of this book is usually neglected even though it is very important. We've definitely touched on a couple of different points regarding this topic throughout the book but I still think it's important to bring them together and introduce a couple of other important concepts that you might not be aware of as well.

Just like most people, when you see 'user interface' it is very possible that what crosses your mind is the bits of Linux that you can be able to see, and how you generally interact with the tool. When it comes to bash scripts, I personally like to look at them as the structure and layout of the commands within the script as well. The end user can be able to read them well and are usually modified to correspond to the ever changing requirements. That means that the ease with which you, the user, can modify and extend your script is very significant.

Tput

'tput' is basically a command that you can use to control the cursor on your terminal as well as the format of the printed content. While very powerful, it is complex but I will introduce a few basics here and leave you to explore it further on your own. The following is an example printing a message in the middle of the screen:

```
1.  #!/bin/bash
2.  # Print message in center of terminal
3.
4.  cols=$( tput cols )
5.  rows=$( tput lines )
6.
7.  message=$@
8.
9.  input_length=${#message}
10.
11.  half_input_length=$(( $input_length / 2 ))
12.
13.  middle_row=$(( $rows / 2 ))
14.  middle_col=$((( $cols / 2) - $half_input_length ))
15.
16.  tput clear
17.
18.  tput cup $middle_row $middle_col
19.  tput bold
20.  echo $@
21.  tput sgr0
22.  tput cup $( tput lines ) 0
```

Let me break that down for you:

In the fourth line, 'tput cols' informs us of the number of columns the terminal has.

In the fifth line, the 'tput lines' inform us the number of lines or rows the terminal contains.

According to the seventh line, all the command line arguments are to be taken and assigned to a single variable message.

According to the ninth line, you are to find out the number of characters that are in the string message. All the input values had to be assigned to the variable message first as '${#@}' would, then inform the number of command arguments that were there as opposed to the number of characters combined.

In the eleventh line, we want to know what half the string message's length is to be able to center it.

In the thirteenth and fourteenth lines, the place where the message should be placed so that it is centered and calculated.

In the sixteenth line, we see that the terminal will be cleared by 'tput'.

In the eighteenth line, we see that the cursor will be placed at the given row and column by the command 'tput cup'.

In the nineteenth line, everything printed on the screen will be made bold by 'tput bold'.

In the twentieth line, you can see that everything is set up and the message can now be printed.

In line 21, the bold function is switched off by 'tput sgro' along with other changes that may have been made.

In line 22, the prompt is placed right at the bottom of the screen.

```
1.
    ./center_message.sh Hello there
2.
3.
                        4. Hello there
5.
6.
```

You need to note that normally, the clear command will be removed by the first prompt (that is where you can run your script). I've left it here just so that you can be able to see that it was run to get the script started.

With 'tput' and a little creativity, you can be able to create some very interesting effects. That is especially so if you delay actions with the 'sleep' command. Just ensure you use it when it is appropriate though. Usually, just printing the processed data (which means not formatting) is more convenient for you, the user.

Supplying The Data

There are three ways in which you can supply data to a bash script. These include the following:

- As command line arguments

- Read interactively in the course of script execution

- Redirected in as STDIN

Your script can use one or more of these but obviously, you should always aim for convenience.

The command line arguments are great since they'll be retained in your (user's) history, which makes it easy for them to return commands. Command line arguments also tend to be very convenient whenever the user is not running the script directly- for instance, as a cron task, part of another script or and so on.

'Redirected from STDN' is particularly practical when your script behaves like a filter and just modifies or reformats data it is fed with.

Lastly, reading interactively is great when you are not aware of the data that may be needed until the script is running already. For instance, you may have to clarify any suspicious or erroneous input. Ideally, passwords are also asked for this way so that they don't just remain plaint text in the history of the user.

Input Flexibility

Now think about how strict you'll be with supplied data too. The more flexible you'll be able to be, the happier you'll be- as the end user. Just think of anyone supplying a date as an argument. He or she could simply supply the date as follows:

21-04-2019

or

21/04/2019

or

21:04:2019

You could write your script and insist on inputting in only one specific format. This would definitely be the easiest for anyone but potentially inconvenient for an end user. What if he or she wants to input the date as given from another source (or command) that offers it in a different format?

You basically should always aim to make things as convenient for the end user as possible; after all, you'll write it only once but an end user will run it many times.

We are allowed to accommodate multiple formats with the 'sed' command for input data.

```
#!/bin/bash
# A date is the first command line argument


clean_date=$( echo $1 | sed 's/[ /:\^#]/-/g' )


echo $clean_date
```

Presenting Data

Don't forget that the terminal and the kind of commands you basically use there are usually a bit different from your usual interaction with computers in the ordinary graphical user interface. Again, you want what's most convenient for the user. Usually, this is only to print out the output as a plain result, without any fancy messages or formatting surrounding it. It is then easiest for the user to redirect the output into other commands for more processing or to a file to be saved.

Organizing code

So far, I think you do understand how important presentation of your code is; you should take pride in it. A good structure makes it simpler for you to see what code is doing and is more difficult to make silly mistakes (which can lead you to wasting too much time quite easily or even worse, if you don't detect the mistake).

I wouldn't be surprised if you took the common approach of *'oh well, I don't make such silly mistakes- I'm too good for that. I can therefore be lazy and write careless code and it will not have or bring any problems.'* Everyone on earth is prone to mistakes. You need to take your time to structure your code properly and later on, you'll thank yourself for doing so.

Indent the code and have it spaced out properly so that the different sections are distinguished easily.

Name the functions and variables with descriptive terms so that what they represent or do is very clear.

So far, you've learnt more than enough when it comes to using the Linux command line as a beginner. This topic is not complete yet, but the hardest part is. Your job now is to practice and test what we've discussed before you brag about your bash skills. Let's see what that's all about:

Testing Your Bash Skills

Usually, we learn as well as remember commands in Linux with greater ease if we actually use them more often in a live scenario. This means that you should practice and use Linux commands often so that you don't forget them like most beginners do.

Whether you are new to this or already are an intermediate user, there are some exciting methods you can use to actually put your bash skills to test. In this section, we are going to look at games. You will test your skills by playing interesting command line games.

Technically though, these are not your every day games like Need for Speed, Counterstrike, Super TuxKart and the like. These are "gamified" versions of command training exercises for Linux. You'll follow certain instructions in the game itself and complete a task.

We'll take a look at a two exciting games that will assist you in learning and practicing Linux commands real-time.

Remember: these are not some of those mind-boggling or time-passing games; they are designed to give you a hands-on experience of terminal commands.

Let's begin.

1. War games

Wargames is an online game, which means that you need to have a good, active internet connection to play. It is a collection of shell games, with each one of them containing many levels. You can only access the subsequent levels by solving the previous levels. The best thing about them is that each one offers clear and concise instructions about the way you can access the subsequent levels. To play the game, follow the link below:

(http://overthewire.org/wargames/)

You'll see something like this:

As you can see, there are many shell games listed on the left side, and each one of them contains its own SSH (secure shell) port. SSH is a network protocol that is used for operating network services over an unsecured network securely. You will thus have to connect to the game through SSH from your local system. Nonetheless, you can find all the details about how to connect each game using SSH in the top-left corner of the game's website.

Let's take an example: we'll play one of the games called Bandit.

Click on the link labelled Bandit on the Wargames homepage to see the SSH information of that particular game.

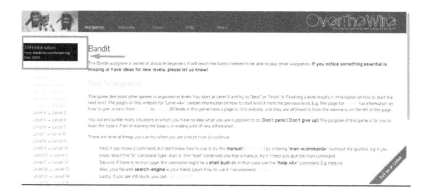

As you can see in the screenshot above, there are many levels. To get to each level, simply click the respective link on the left column. You'll find instructions there for beginners on the right side. Make sure you read them if you have any questions about the game.

Now go to 'level 0' by clicking on it.

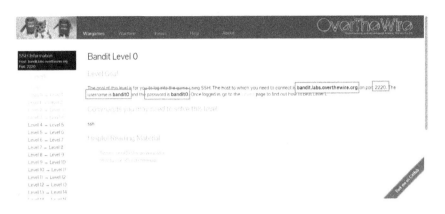

Connect to Bandit game level 0 using the information provided above:

$ ssh bandit0@bandit.labs.overthewire.org -p 2220

Enter 'bandit0' as the password:

The output will be something like this:

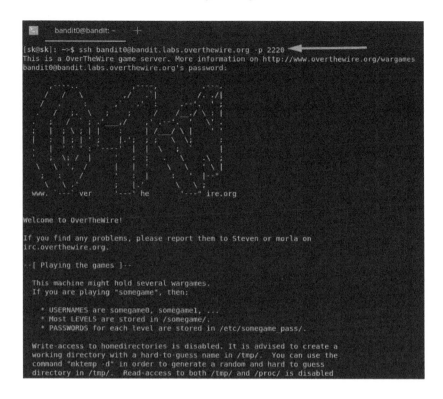

When you are logged in, type the command 'Is' to see what's available or simply go to the 'level 1' page to learn how to beat level 1 and so on. The list of every command has been given in each level. Therefore, you can thus pick and use any command you find suitable to go through each level. I have to warn you though: wargames are quite addictive because each level is really fun and unique. However, some levels are very challenging but it's really worth your time.

2. The "clmystery" game

Unlike the game above, this game can be played locally; you don't have to connect your system to a remote system.

Clymystery is a very interesting game that involves you, the user, playing detective to solve a mystery incident by simply following the given instructions in the game.

The first thing you have to do is clone the repository as follows:

$ git clone https://github.com/veltman/clmystery.git

Alternatively, you can download it as a zip file using the link below:

https://github.com/veltman/clmystery/archive/master.zip

Extract the game and go to the location where the files are contained. When you do that, solve the mystery case by reading the instructions:

[sk@sk]: clmystery-master>$ ls

cheatsheet.md cheatsheet.pdf encoded hint1 hint2 hint3 hint4 hint5 hint6 hint7 hint8 instructions LICENSE.md mystery README.md solution

Now use the following instructions/information to play the game:

There is a city by the name Terminal in which a murder has occurred. The Terminal City Police Department (TCPD) need your help to figure out who the culprit is.

To discover the person who did it, first go to the subdirectory named 'mystery' and begin working from there. You might have to look into all the clues at the crime scene (that's the 'crimescene' file). The officers, at the crime scene, as you will discover, are very meticulous, as they've jotted everything in their reports. You also need to know that the sergeant went through the real clues and marked them out using the word 'clue' in all the caps.

In case you get stuck anywhere, simply open one of the hint files (for instance, hint1, hint 2 and so on). You can also open these files using the command file like so:

$ cat hint1

If you want to check the answer or know the solution, you can simply open the file labelled 'solution' in the clmystery directory.

($ cat solution)

Conclusion

Okay, so you've worked through my book. Congratulations! You have learnt all you need to learn to become a perfect Linux command line ninja. You have acquired powerful and really practical skills and knowledge. What remains is a little experience. Undoubtedly, your bash scripting is reasonably good now but like I mentioned, you have to practice to perfect it.

This book was meant to introduce you to Linux and the Linux command line right from scratch, teach you what you need to know to use it properly and a bit more to take you to the next level. At this point, I can say that you are on your way to doing something great with bash, so don't hang your boots just yet.

www.ingramcontent.com/pod-product-compliance
Lightning Source LLC
Chambersburg PA
CBHW021143070326
40689CB00043B/1107